Including Childre
Attention and Behaviou
in the Foundation Stage

Written by
Maureen Garner

Edited by
Sally Featherstone

Illustrated by
Martha Hardy

First published 2010 by A&C Black Publishers Limited
This third edition published by Featherstone, an imprint of Bloomsbury Publishing Plc
50 Bedford Square, London WC1B 3DP
www.bloomsbury.com

ISBN 978-1-4729-0657-1

Text © Maureen Garner, 2005
Illustrations © Martha Hardy

Printed and bound in Great Britain by CPI Group (UK) Ltd, Croydon CRO 4YY

1 3 5 7 9 10 8 6 4 2

This book is produced using paper that is made from wood grown in
managed, sustainable forests. It is natural, renewable and recyclable.
The logging and manufacturing processes conform to the environmental
regulations of the country of origin.

**To see our full range of titles
visit www.bloomsbury.com**

Contents

Introduction   **4**

Key facts and questions   **6**

Could this be ADHD?   6

Dispelling myths   7

Other reasons for difficult behaviour   8

Making the best of starts   9

The other side of the fence   11

Questions parents may ask   13

Expectations   **14**

Helping the child   14

More about expectations   15

Stages of development   16

How behaviour can affect learning in the EYFS Curriculum   **21**

Personal, social and emotional development   21

Communication and language   22

Developing key skills and strategies   **25**

Possible reasons for unwanted behaviour   25

Helping children to behave well   26

Setting achievable targets   28

Ideas for managing behaviour in groups   29

A purposeful programme   **31**

Identifying and using targets   31

Singing their praises   32

Changing a child's behaviour   33

What is Time Out and how does it work?   39

Focus on observation   41

The ABC of behaviour management   43

Strategies for specific behaviours   45

Case Studies   **50**

Partnership with parents   **57**

Working as a member of a team   **59**

Who's who in multi-agency working?   **61**

Further help and key contacts   **63**

Resources and websites   **64**

Introduction

The Early Years Foundation stage (EYFS) is a time when all young children are offered opportunities to be active learners, to be partners in play and to imagine, create and explore. It allows them to work, develop and progress at their own pace and is ideally suited to meet the individual needs of all children.

This book can help you to make the most of the Early Years Foundation stage for young children who experience behavioural and/or attention difficulties. It aims to encourage, reassure and inspire you in your efforts to help these children to develop as individuals and to make good progress in spite of their difficulties.

This book will:

Although this book is predominantly for Early Years practitioners, it will also be useful for parents and anyone else wanting to support young children. The practical ideas and strategies can be easily adapted or modified to the individual needs of the child, at home or in a group setting, as well as being used for children without speech and language delay.

Inform you by:

- providing essential information about behaviour and attention difficulties
- signposting you to further resources
- telling you about the effects of behaviour and attention difficulties on learning
- helping you with different approaches and ways of working.

Support you by:

- giving advice about ways of working with support staff
- helping you to contribute to a multi agency team
- suggesting practical strategies for behaviour management
- giving practical strategies for dealing with difficulties as they arise
- offering tried and tested tips.

Inspire you by:

- giving insight into the parent's perspective
- suggesting innovative ideas for activities
- describing ways of making a smooth start to the Foundation Stage.

Make you think by asking:

- How does it feel to have difficulties of behaviour which may cause people to dislike or avoid you?
- What is it like to feel different?
- What is it like to be the parent of a child with behavioural difficulties?
- How can you help other children to deal with the problems this may create?

Make you ask yourself some hard questions such as:

- How can I make a real relationship with this child?
- How can I make him/her feel good about himself/herself?
- What do I need to do for and with this child to help them make the most of the Early Years Foundation Stage?
- How can I help children understand, value, support and accept each other?
- How can I learn to understand the behaviour so I don't get upset, hurt or find myself taking things personally?

Who is this book for?

This book is for anyone interested in helping very young children to manage their own behaviour. It will also interest students and Early Years practitioners. Many of the suggestions are adaptations of activities suitable for all children whether or not they have difficulties, and should therefore be useful for the encouragement of positive behaviour in all children in the Early Years Foundation stage.

The activity and ideas pages:

These pages are:

- packed with simple ideas which do not require special resources
- based on opportunities to reinforce good behaviour
- full of ideas to improve attention
- planned to help children to get on with each other and to respond appropriately to adult attention
- written to take account of different learning styles and particularly the 'small steps' approach which results in the satisfaction of achievement and frequent reward.

Key facts and questions

Could this be ADHD?

All young children are very active; they have lots of energy to burn and are always 'on the go'. Play, movement and physical activity are central to early learning, so it is very unusual for a child to be diagnosed with ADHD at this early age, and in the Early Years Foundation Stage all children need to be offered as many outlets for their physical energy as possible.

Although ADHD symptoms may start as early as the age of three, many of the symptoms are within the normal range of behaviour in such young children, so formal diagnosis is rarely made before the age of seven. It is therefore better to try the ideas in this book before rushing to a diagnosis of ADHD!

Some children with ADHD are inattentive:

- they are easily distracted

- they repeatedly fail to finish tasks

- they have poor concentration

- they daydream.

> **Is it ADHD, ADD or is it within the normal range of behaviour for very young children?**

Some children with ADHD are hyperactive or impulsive:

- they may wriggle, squirm and fidget constantly

- they may be unable to take turns or wait

- they may act impulsively without thought for consequences.

These children are often quite capable of paying attention, and they are most commonly under the age of 6.

Some children with ADHD have a combination of inattention and hyperactivity:

- they show signs of both types of behaviour described above, and are more commonly of an older age.

Some children with attention difficulties are not hyperactive and are often girls. They are sometimes described as having ADD, or Attention Deficit Disorder.

The behaviours described above will sound familiar to Early Years practitioners; they are typical of many young children and this is what makes diagnosis so difficult. However, a child with ADD/ADHD will have more extreme symptoms than most. This child will be more easily distracted and more impulsive. At times, activity levels can be almost frenetic. For a diagnosis of ADHD to be made, these symptoms must be present for at least 6 months and must have a negative effect on the child's life both at home and in school, and affect socialisation and making friends. Three times as many boys as girls are affected and there is sometimes a strong family history of behaviour problems.

Dispelling myths!

ADHD is not caused by poor parenting, family difficulties, too much TV or bad teaching; and although some young children are undoubtedly affected by food additives, this applies to no more than 5% of ADHD sufferers.

It is not proven that ADHD is caused by 'minimal brain damage', head injury or a difficult birth. However, use of brain imaging techniques, such as MRI has recently shown that there are significant differences between ADHD patients and individuals who do not have ADHD. Studies of MRI scans have shown that children who have ADHD have under-active parts of the brain, when involved in certain activities. You cannot make this diagnosis yourself; it must be made by a team of specialists including paediatricians and psychologists.

If you have significant concerns that a child has a problem:

- inform the manager or head of your setting

- discuss your concerns with parents who should be encouraged to consult their own doctor.

It is also a good idea to:

- consult the advisory teachers and other support workers from the EYDCP for your area.

and, if necessary:

- discuss a referral to the local Educational Psychologist.

> Remember that diagnosing ADHD is a specialist task which takes time and experience. Don't rush to judgement.

Above all, never label a child, keep their parents informed and involved at all stages and remember that a diagnosis does not change the child or the needs. He/she is still an individual, who has the right to be loved and cared for, to have their needs met and to be given every opportunity to learn and develop in their own way, at their own pace, and to the very best of their ability.

Specialists now suspect that ADD/ADHD is considerably under-diagnosed, so it is very important that if you have real concerns about a child that you talk to their parents and make sure that they ask for referral to a paediatrician who will undertake any necessary investigations.

There are many people who can help you with the difficulties the child may have, and it is usually felt that a combination of drug therapy, behaviour modification, and psychological intervention is the best way forward in many cases. While awaiting the results of any of this treatment, you will have to deal with the child in the setting, and remember you are not a medical expert.

Maintain a professional approach:

- Don't panic, stay calm.
- Don't take the behaviour personally.
- Don't label, don't blame.
- Don't try random ideas or things you have seen on TV.
- Do talk to parents.
- Do watch the child carefully so you have objective information.
- Don't assume it is ADHD.

Other reasons for difficult behaviour

Children who have behaviour difficulties may be suffering from one (or more) of a variety of conditions. For instance:

- they may have an Autistic Spectrum Disorder (ASD), in which case there will be other difficulties apparent. Children with ASD should be diagnosed by a paediatrician and/ or psychologist. Children on the autistic spectrum may respond to the ideas and methods in this book, but you need to understand that a child with autism has a disorder over which they have no control. You will need to learn about autism, and get specialist advice on how to deal with the problems it presents.

- a few children may be suffering from one of a range of other disorders, difficulties, syndromes and disabilities.

> **Examples of syndromes with associated behaviour difficulties are:**
> **Prader Willi Syndrome, Turner's Syndrome, Hurler's Syndrome (and other conditions of mucopolysaccharide origin), obsessive compulsive disorder, Tourette's Syndrome.**

If you have concerns about any child, ask their parents for information and use the local network of advice available in your area to find out more about the difficulties the child is displaying. You will need to find out something about the condition before you try to eliminate the problems you are experiencing. Some conditions are so complex that elimination of behaviour and attention difficulties may not be possible, but careful teaching and sympathetic handling may help children to manage their own behaviour within the limitations of their complex syndromes. Use expert help, look for information, contact local and national support groups, and above all, work at developing a good, honest and open relationship with the child's parents.

The group of children who have a permanent disorder, leading to problematic, 'difficult to handle' behaviour is very small. Most of the children we meet will not have such difficulties, but may from time to time show or develop behaviours which they need help to overcome.

Check other possibilities, and don't rush to judgement. Use all your skills and experience to look at the problem yourself.

Difficult behaviour is often a cry for help when a child is finding something difficult to handle on their own. Remember, he/she is not trying to be more difficult than usual, just trying to come to terms with difficulties, and we are the ones who sometimes find it hard to manage.

Making the best of starts

- If you know of a difficulty before the child arrives at your setting, make sure you arrange a home visit when you are not under the pressure of time.

- Encourage the parent/carer to tell you about their child, what they are hoping for and what their fears and worries are. Make some brief notes during or just after the visit.

- Remember to listen as well as talk. Parents may be shy, anxious or worried, or even ashamed of their child's behaviour.

- Explain about the key person role and how it works. Arrange a meeting with the key person who will be the consistent contact with the family.

- Play with the child's own toys as well as any you take with you. Don't make it look like a test, rather a 'get to know you session'.

- Reassure parents that their child can bring an object from home to give them comfort. A favourite cup or toy can provide a real link.

- Plan together how the first few days can be made reassuring. If you are aware of possible problems before the child starts at your setting, you will be prepared to avoid difficulties.

- Explain carefully what you will be providing for their child and how you will plan to ensure that their child's needs will be met. Make sure parents can meet the special needs co-ordinator and find out about their role and responsibilities. Provide key contact numbers.

- Find out about any other professionals or workers who are in contact with the family. These could include volunteers, representatives of national or local support groups, health visitors, Early Years advisers, parents of other children with the same problems etc. Ask the parents before you contact them, and get parental permission to arrange any meetings.

- Talk about self-help skills and working together for independence.

- Explain the behaviour policy of your setting, emphasising the importance of positive reinforcement and encouraging acceptable behaviour rather than punishing unwanted behaviour.

> **Talk, listen, find out, ask questions, collect all the information you can. Make contact with agencies and others who have contact with the child and family.**

- Agree which are the most important behaviours to tackle first, and which might safely be left until later.

- Make sure parents understand that you can't tackle everything at once and that being consistent at home and in school is vital.

- Help parents to understand that they may need to change some of their own behaviour, but without making them feel guilty or responsible for their child's difficulties.

- Leave some photographs of the setting to show the child where they are going to be and the people they will meet.

- Arrange at least one, and preferably more visits to your setting, so the child and his/her carers can get to know the people they will be with and the places they will be.

And when you get back to your setting:

- Discuss the key features of your meeting with the family. Remember not to encourage panic or judgement in your colleagues!

- Make sure you have done all you can to help all staff to welcome the child as a valued individual.

- Make sure that everyone knows what sort of behaviours may occur, and how you have agreed they will be dealt with. Remember consistency is vital! Ensure that everyone knows about and uses positive reinforcement techniques.

- Tell everyone about the behaviour(s) you have agreed to work on first. Make sure everyone knows what to do about other behaviours if they occur.

- Give the child plenty of time to settle in, but be clear about routines and expectations from the start.

The other side of the fence

Imagine being the parent whose child is never invited to parties.

Imagine being the one who invites children to play but no one will come.

Imagine being the mum of the loneliest child in the school, the child who is blamed for everything that goes wrong, sometimes even for someone else's poor behaviour, or even when they weren't there!

Imagine being afraid to go to school at the end of the day because you dread what you will be told this time. Imagine not only that no one else likes your child, but that some of the time you are not even sure that you like him or her yourself!

How would you feel if you were the parent of that boy or girl?

This may sound like some dreadful nightmare, but it is often what happens to the parents of a child whose difficulties are behavioural. If a child has an obvious disability, like Down's Syndrome, or something which everyone has at least heard of, then people will make allowances, feel sympathy and try to understand. But a behaviour problem is not always perceived as a disability, just a child 'playing up', 'out of control' or 'not brought up properly'. Parent and child are condemned for the behaviour.

Being the mum or dad of a difficult child can be a soul destroying process. It takes away your self esteem, your confidence in yourself as a parent and your chance to make friends of the other parents at the school gate. You feel that everyone is blaming you for the way your child behaves and that they think you both need punishment.

You may have been struggling alone for a long time, not managing to change your child's behaviour and being too ashamed to ask for help. You may have been denying to yourself that there is a problem and hoping that when your child goes to school or nursery he/she will improve, copy the others, or learn to behave 'properly'. Parents in this situation need help and understanding, not condemnation.

Parents may not have had good models of parenting themselves, they may have had time in trouble, their own experiences of school may have been unhappy ones. They may have been a difficult child themselves, and have more sympathy with their child's feelings and actions than we do. Parents will naturally be on the defensive, and may therefore come over as aggressive. Try to understand that this is very natural and needs sensitive handling.

Remember, it is not only you who is trying to manage the child. The parents have them too, and for much longer hours than you do. They may not be able to send their child to someone else for an hour or so, or to get much 'time off'. In situations like this, the parent needs just as much help and support as the child and will be delighted to have someone who is supportive to them, listens and tries to understand.

A parent may deny that there are any problems with behaviour at home. They may feel that it is all to do with the way you are running your setting. This again is natural (and may even be true!). Parents will want to defend their child, and their own self esteem. Explain that you are experiencing difficulties and that you need their help to deal with the problem. Help them to understand that their advice is vital to you, and you would like yours to be valuable to them. Parents know their child much better than you, so enlist their help and work together.

All parents feel anxious when their child needs to move to a new stage in their life – starting school or nursery, even moving to a new class. Events such as these are even more worrying for a parent who is not only concerned about how their child will cope, but dreads that the change may make the behaviour even worse.

Questions parents may ask

Parents may need to ask questions such as:

- Will my child be able to cope?

- Will they make friends?

- How will other parents react?

- Have I been doing the right things?

- Do you really want my child here?

- Do you think I am a bad parent?

Some may want to ask these questions but be afraid to!

The list will be different for every parent. They may also worry and not ask:

- What will happen if they hurt another child?

- What will happen if they can't sit still, can't conform, can't understand instructions?

- What will happen if they have a temper tantrum?

- What will happen if they run away/ throw things/ swear/ damage equipment/ climb/ hide under the table/ hit an adult?

And this means these parents will probably need:

- more support than others at the time their child starts to attend your setting, or when their difficulties become apparent

- regular positive encouragement and clear goals

- honest and focused feedback

- regular contact with the child's key person

- good news every time their child has behaved well or achieved a target

- not to be given the bad news every day, but a balanced and honest view of their child's achievements and problems.

Expectations

Helping the child

Children who have problems with their behaviour need to feel that they are valued for themselves and their contributions to school life.

- They may not be used to dealing with the kind of boundaries that you set and may need more help to come to terms with these.

- They may be used to getting their own way by tantrums and fighting authority and need to be shown alternatives.

- They may be the one in charge at home and will need to learn how to conform to a different situation with you.

> **Nobody pretends this is easy!**
>
> **If it was easy we wouldn't need to write this book!**

- They may be used to gaining attention with poor behaviour and will need to understand that good behaviour gets positive attention and that poor behaviour gets no attention at all (or as little as possible).

You need to strike a balance between ensuring that a child gets the attention he/she needs, and giving him/her the opportunity to manage their own behaviour while playing alongside others.

- They may need more reminders and guidance to help them understand and conform to the rules and routines of your setting.

- They will need to see that others are praised and rewarded for their achievements and that they will take part in these celebrations when they do well.

- Some children like their praise to be private and low key, others love a public display. Find out how they like to receive their recognition.

> **Be clear about expectations, catch them getting behaviour right!**

- Be clear that every child is an individual and it is their individual achievements which are celebrated, not how they measure up to other children.

Try not to make comparisons with other children when recognising achievements or problems.

> **Use the power of praise, not the weapon of comparison.**

More about expectations

It is important to be realistic in your expectations of children's behaviour. If you are unrealistic, children will not be able to do what you expect of them and conflicts will almost certainly result.

If a child has never enjoyed a book with their family, we should not expect them to sit on a carpet with a large group of other children for twenty minutes for a story. If a child is allowed to go to bed leaving all his toys scattered around the floor to be put away later by mum, then they may not understand the concept of tidying up.

Remember:

- Most children want to be good! They want to be praised, liked and treated as someone who is valued.

- Behaviour is not necessarily 'naughty' just because it does not conform to our idea of what is 'good'. Some children are just confused about what the rules are!

- Young children do not usually set out to be difficult. It is the adult who finds the behaviour difficult, not the child.

- There is usually a reason why the behaviour occurs. That reason may be unconscious, hidden or triggered by something which has just happened, or even happened some time ago.

- Changes in routine or in the happenings in a child's life can cause major changes in behaviour. Some examples are:

  - the arrival of a new baby

  - moving house

  - starting school/nursery

  - changes in family relationships

  - illness

  - lack of sleep

  - changes in childcare arrangements

  - loss of any kind, e.g. loss of a significant adult through death or separation

  - even the loss of a favourite toy.

Most children want to be good!

Look for the reason behind the behaviour.

These events and experiences are part of the child, so remember to find out about the events in children's lives, take such things into account and give sensitive consideration to their possible effects on a child's behaviour.

Encourage parents to let you know of key events which may affect a child so you can anticipate and avoid difficulties before they arise.

Stages of Development

Accepting both the age of a child and the stage of their development is a vital component in the management of behaviour. If we know the usual range of behavioural development in children of a particular age or developmental stage, then we are more likely to have reasonable expectations of them.

Understanding child development is vital to the process of helping children whose behaviour may not follow the norm. These children often have a wider discrepancy than usual between their age and their current stage of development (for instance a five year old may be behaviourally at a three year old stage of development).

Child Development

The development of behaviour is even more varied than the development of physical growth, and is affected by many factors. These include:

- a child's individual temperament and characteristics

- the context of his/her family

- the cultural and social environment and the expectations within it

- whether the child has learning or physical difficulties, or any other special needs which could delay or alter development

- their gender (boys often develop later than girls).

Individual children develop at very different rates, and we must not become concerned too quickly or make a referral when development does not occur at a specific time. Children usually follow a pattern closely related to their age, structured markers only give general guidance, and there are always exceptions!

The following descriptions show what might be expected at different ages. We have given chronological ages for guidance, beginning at the stage between 1 and 2 years. The notes extend to cover 6-7 year old development, to cover the characteristics of children beyond the Foundation Stage.

Most children at twelve months:

- do not understand that they are a separate person

- like to be with the people they know well, and may be upset with strangers

- respond in different ways at different times to similar situations; they may laugh at a rough and tumble game one day and be upset by it the next

- can follow a simple instruction, such as 'Come to Mummy'

- make sounds, call and shout to gain attention.

By 15 months, children are usually:

- more aware of themselves, but don't yet understand that others are separate beings

- into everything, exploring without any idea of what it is safe to do and touch

- very possessive, particularly of people he/she loves. For instance, they do not like to see Mum/Dad holding another baby

- easily distracted from behaviours that are unwanted; trying to reason with him/her will not work very well. Moods swing from joy to fury in seconds

- easily frustrated and this sometimes results in shouting and throwing things.

By 18 months, a child is usually:

- more aware of him/herself as distinct from others

- responsive (briefly) to being told 'no', but needs it to be repeated frequently, reinforced by actions such as picking them up and moving them away from danger at the same time as saying 'no'

- totally self-centred, unconcerned about the effect of their actions on others

- very determined to have their own way, easily frustrated at not being able to do things for themselves, and resistant to being stopped by someone else.

By 18 months, a child sometimes:

- responds to frustration by throwing, screaming or shouting

- tries to assert him/herself by refusing to comply with adults and showing defiance.

A 2 year old:

- has a clearer self-image, but still does not appreciate others as separate people
- is able to play alone for up to 20 minutes, as long as they know a trusted adult is nearby
- is very possessive of their own toys - everything is 'mine'. Sharing has not yet become a way of life, and needs to be treated as a developmental stage and not a punishable offence. He/she needs to be shown how to share by frequent and sensitive adult intervention
- does not like to wait for demands to be met, impatience is normal
- will have frequent tantrums when frustrated, even if you are not aware of the cause; can usually be distracted, but you need to guard against rewarding them for screaming by giving your attention
- is now able to show and express feelings, of affection, fear, anger, distress
- can now understand when others are upset, hurt, excited or happy and will respond appropriately.

A 3 year old:

- knows him/herself well and is becoming increasingly independent
- is often resistant to being told what to do and how to do it, usually thinking they know best!
- will go happily with people they know, and is much less worried about strangers, becoming more sociable and less shy
- has usually developed the ability to wait when necessary
- is willing to discuss what he/she needs to do, and to negotiate appropriate behaviours and responses
- usually has a good command of language and therefore is less likely to have a tantrum or behave rebelliously
- has sudden mood swings and sometimes behaves in extreme ways without necessarily knowing the reason why
- likes to be seen to be well behaved, and knows what to do when taken into a wide range of social situations
- is able to appreciate what is going on around him/her and to fit in with the feelings and moods of adults around him/her
- has a real need for approval. Wants to be loved and appreciated by adults.

A typical 4 year old:

- can take part in discussions, negotiate and reason

- is very friendly and can be helpful to both other children and adults

- understands their own feelings and is therefore more likely to respond in a predictable way and to express feelings verbally

- is much more self-controlled and can control bodily movements well

- is less dependent on the main carer and likes to do things with other adults

- is mostly able to behave appropriately in different situations, understanding what to do where and when

- likes to play in a small group, not necessarily with friends, but with those showing an interest in the same activity; he/she can move between groups happily and independently

- takes turns in group games with other children, but usually needs an adult to keep the structure of the game and ensure consistency

- enjoys imaginative play, and can continue for considerable lengths of time with complicated ideas

- understands yesterday, today and tomorrow, as well as now, before, later

- will argue the case and put their own ideas quite strongly

- sometimes blames others for their own misbehaviour and denies their own part in it; this is part of a need for approval and a growing awareness of consequences

- will sometimes behave badly as a way to gain a reaction from an adult. Any attention can be seen as better than none

- may swear and use forbidden language, again as a way to gain attention.

During the year between 4 and 5:

- although they may seem very confident, sociable and talkative, children are trying to make sense of the world and their part in it
- self-assurance develops and activities are more purposeful
- children are more inclined to follow a thing through to the end
- being able to wait, take turns and to share with others is so much part of behaviour that they no longer need to think about it
- children are sometimes stubborn, argumentative and aggressive with adults and other children
- a child who is unwell or tired still needs the help and security of a trusted adult.

A typical 5 year old:

- is more independent, more self-contained and more self-controlled
- needs the approval of adults to support their self-esteem
- knows, and feel ashamed when their behaviour is unacceptable
- will sometimes be overactive, aggressive and argumentative
- will argue with parents, but not usually with teachers or other adults when denied something
- will engage in negotiation and bargaining; this is still useful as a way of ensuring good behaviour
- is not so easily distracted from anger or frustration
- needs to be given ways to regain control when angry; 'Time Out' usually helps
- enjoys games which enable them to be competitive as individuals rather than in teams
- still needs adult intervention to adjudicate in arguments
- likes to assert themselves by boasting and sometimes threatening others
- loves to be the best and can be very purposeful and persistent to achieve this.

During the year between 6 and 7:

- children show an increasing level of maturity and independence
- their emotions and behaviour are developing to suit the situations and social settings in which they find themselves
- they can be friendly, co-operative and self-confident
- spells of irritability, sulkiness and rebellion are still part of their nature.

How behaviour can affect learning in the EYFS Curriculum

Personal, social and emotional development

Personal, social and emotional development is the area of the curriculum which may present the highest challenge to a child with difficulties of behaviour and attention. Having difficulties in this area will naturally make a great deal of difference to the way children learn, because they need personal and interpersonal skills to achieve in all the other areas. Concentration, comprehension and self-esteem are vital.

Each child is different, and some will have difficulties with making relationships, separating from parents/carers and conforming to new conditions and experiences.

Most children will respond well to new situations and challenges but some will need extra help and support.

A child with difficulties in these areas will need extra help to:

- listen well, pay attention, respond to verbal requests or instructions
- follow the rules in simple games
- follow the normal routine of the setting
- take turns and cope with sharing both equipment and people
- develop friendships.

Children with these difficulties may find some parts of the routine more challenging. Remember, they are not being deliberately difficult; they are learning how to behave in activities which they may have not met before. Most children will learn, by observation and encouragement, what is expected of them in areas such as:

- circle and story times, or activities requiring sitting quietly in a group situation
- imaginative play
- table play with books, puzzles etc.
- responding to verbal instructions.

Children with attention difficulties may need additional support to make the most of the opportunities being offered to them, and to learn to conform to the expectations of your setting.

Communication and Language

Many children with behaviour and attention difficulties have good language skills. Their spoken language is often as good as that of their peers. But they may well have difficulties with the processing of language and making full sense of what they are being asked.

Children with ADD may have had poor models of spoken language at home; they may be used to shouting and inappropriate language; they may have seen unacceptable behaviour in the adults around them. They may not be used to using language for thinking and reasoning and will be working within the earlier stages in the Foundation Stage Guidance. Some children may need time to learn more appropriate ways of using the language they have acquired. Making a trusting and open relationship with parents will help! Give them the opportunity to see and hear you working with both their own and other children, explain the need to use language to help the child co-operate, as well as the need for constant praise and reinforcement. This will help parents to help their own children.

Build relationships.

Visual clues, such as pictures, objects, signs or a demonstration alongside the verbal instruction will provide children with a 'prop' to help their understanding of what you expect.

Use visual clues and cues.

A child may have a short-term auditory memory problem – the memory used to hold, process and assimilate spoken language. This will have implications for their ability to listen, recall and act upon the spoken word.

It may also affect the way in which children learn to use new words and later on the way they learn to read. Short term memory problems may affect a child's response to your requests, and their behaviour in the setting. Although a short-term auditory memory problem will not account completely for a child's behaviour and attention difficulties, it is always worth considering.

Help them improve short term memory.

You can make a real difference to a child's working or short term memory by:

- playing listening and memory games (individually and in small groups)

- providing visual clues and prompts

- using routine and set sequences in games

- using music, rhythm and song

- making the child aware of when they need to stop, focus and listen

- reducing background and competing noise to help listening

- giving information in small chunks instead of complicated sentences.

Remember the importance of working in a small group to help individuals know you are focusing on them, and care about them. Pretend play and many other everyday play activities provide the ideal vehicle for children to expand their language skills individually and alongside other children.

Small step targets in this area should include:

Small groups work!

- listening skills
- understanding language
- memory and recall
- social interaction, such as sharing and turn taking.

When developing writing skills don't expect too much of a child too soon. Mark making skills follow a well accepted sequence. Don't move too quickly on to letter formation before they have full control of their hands and understand what pencils, crayons and paint can do. This is a sure way to create confusion and frustration!

A child who has difficulty controlling behaviour, who then fails to get the positive feedback he craves, is likely to respond with an outburst. Not only will he have to manage his feelings of failure, but those of disapproval and disappointment both in you and himself. It is absolutely imperative to ensure that every child is given tasks which are well matched and within their grasp, which they are totally ready for and understand thoroughly. Observe before you decide the level of activity, this will help all children, not only the ones who have behaviour difficulties.

Practice and variety are essential. Make sure all children have plenty of time for repetition and practice at each stage with different materials. These children will need to gain confidence as well as competence. Sometimes using a child's own interests is a good way to start.

When planning activities, consider:

- what motivates and interests the child
- his/her level of understanding and ability to co-operate
- the child's preferred learning style
- his/her ability to listen and attend.

Books and learning to read

Many children will come to the Foundation Stage with a wonderful experience of books at home, a rich background of bedtime stories and all the joys that books can bring. Others are not so fortunate, and these may be the ones whose behaviour and attention skills have been slow to develop. Perhaps the early signs of an attention disorder meant they could not sit still for a story and their busy parents have given up trying. Some of these children will not come swiftly and naturally to reading.

Take notice of what parents are saying. Talk about the child's previous interest in and experience of stories, nursery rhymes and books. Parents may be reluctant to say that they have not told their child stories – because they know you think it's important! Take time to build up trust and confidence.

If a child has had little or no opportunity to develop early literacy skills, you may have to start at an early stage. Work with the family to help them to learn about books. Use library and loan collections, and encourage short, enjoyable sessions at home, slowly extending expectations and their attention span.

Praise, praise and more praise is the thing. Giving a child praise, love and a continued sense of their own worth and self esteem is the way to improve attention, concentration, and behaviour. Use and encourage the power of praise!

> **Use and encourage the power of praise!**

Developing key skills and strategies

Possible reasons for unwanted behaviour

- Curiosity – children are naturally curious. This is how they learn about the world and we naturally encourage them to explore and experiment. But children are not always able to know what is acceptable exploration, and what isn't, and they don't always understand that what they were asked to do yesterday isn't on the agenda for today.

- Imitation – again, this is a way in which children learn, and they will imitate what we don't want them to do as well as what we do. Don't forget, they will imitate you as well, so watch your own behaviour!

- Sense of self – young children do not easily see things from another's point of view and may therefore be unfair or unkind without meaning to be. They do not yet appreciate that what hurts them will also hurt others. This behaviour needs understanding, modelling and time to change. Be clear about the behaviour you don't like, and why you don't like it.

- Independence – children want to make their own decisions and do things by and for themselves. Of course we want them to learn independence, but some children can't set reasonable limits, and need our help.

- Attention seeking – children learn from experience. If their experience tells them that if they are good they are ignored, and if they are not, they will get attention, then that is what they will do – and so will many others!

- Anger and frustration – this may be reflected in anti-social ways, throwing or physical violence against others. Young children do not understand, and are not yet able to control strong emotions. They hit out until they are shown other ways to react, and are mature enough to manage them.

- Boredom – If there is nothing interesting to do a child may use their own initiative to think up something that is!

- Testing (how far they can go) – Again, this is a very necessary part of the child's maturation process. All children test our consistency and limits!

- Unrealistic demands – sometimes children are not physically or emotionally capable of the behaviours expected of them. Know each child as an individual; don't expect them to do a thing just because another child can.

- Unaware of the behaviour expected of them – this often occurs when the expectations at home or in another setting are not the same as in yours. Sometimes, young children do not realise that instructions given to the whole group are intended for them as well. Make sure you are clear in your messages. Repeat instructions and guidance.

- Not used to doing as they are told – many parents do not insist on a child doing what he is told, and will give in if the child does not comply at once. Mixed messages are confusing and you need to find a way of helping children and parents to make expectations clear.

- Tiredness or illness – this often results in a child responding in an unusual way or being 'snappy' before you are aware of the reason.

- Anxiety or fear – a change in behaviour is often a symptom of emotional upset, a change of circumstances, either at home or in the setting.

Helping children to behave well

There is much that can be done to help children to manage those things which do not come naturally to them. It is extremely important not to make the child feel that everything they do is wrong, or is their fault.

Try to put yourself in their place – for example, when an instruction is given by the adult:

- Can the child hear the adult? Hearing develops slowly and in fits and starts, especially in boys.

- Is he/she engrossed in an activity which they don't want to leave?

- Is he/she distracted by thinking about or watching something else? Young children, especially boys find it hard to do more than one thing at a time.

- Does he/she find sitting down with lots of others claustrophobic? Some children may have never had a large group experience.

- Has he/she had a bad experience at carpet time (perhaps being hurt by another child, being physically uncomfortable or being repeatedly reprimanded) which makes him/her feel anxious? Watch the child (or ask someone to help) and see if you can find a reason for their behaviour.

There will be other reasons which you, with your knowledge of individual children, will be able to think of. Don't expect to change everything overnight. Discuss the reasons with your colleagues and come up with suggestions to try, both with the whole group and with those individual children who are experiencing difficulties.

> Try modelling behaviours and play activities for them to copy.

Remember that children with difficulties need time and a gentle approach. Observe what the child is doing before you intervene or ask them to do something different.

On a day to day basis remember to:

- make sure you show a child the appropriate way to play with the toys

- try lots of simple games in a small group situation to help children get along with each other

- give instructions with visual prompts - show the child what you want them to do rather than just saying it

- make routines and expectations very clear and consistent. You need to ensure that what you are asking is realistic and achievable for the child

- give instructions one at a time and in simple language. Saying 'Go to the cloakroom and get your coat from the peg, then bring it to Mrs Jones to help you put it on before you go out', will not help a child whose attention or understanding is poor

- giving instructions which you know are easy for the child to achieve will give you more opportunities to use praise and encouragement

- use pictures or objects to help a child understand what is to happen next

- for children who find it difficult to understand or interpret instructions, turn the areas of difficulty into specific targets for the whole setting

- give plenty of warning about changes in activities; try telling them individually that it is almost time to stop, rather than expecting that they will understand that, for instance, the tune we are playing means 'Tidy up time'.

They will eventually learn the usual routine, but may need lots of reinforcement over several weeks before it comes naturally!

Setting achievable targets

All difficulties, whether caused by a lack of maturity, a learning disability or a behavioural problem need to be broken down into a series of small steps, which can be made into targets, and achieved one at a time by the child.

> **Never follow up praise with a negative such as. 'You sat very well at milk time. Why can't you always do that?'**

Achieving one target and being consistently praised for it will have a much more positive effect on a child than having a target which is too large, or too many targets at once. Achieving targets and receiving praise will help to raise their self-esteem. To be told that you have done well today because you came to sit down with every one else at milk time is much better than being told you were naughty because you did not sit down with everyone else at story time, circle time or dinner time.

Accept good behaviour and praise it for what it is, not for what you would like it to be.

Higher self-esteem will help a child to:

- relate to the other children in the group

- make friendships

- see themselves as valued, not the troublesome or naughty child.

> **Use the power of praise, not the weapon of comparison.**

It can be hard to praise a child who does something which you expect to be the norm for all the other children. Try hard not to make comparisons. Recognise that you are helping an individual to achieve a small step on the way to behaving like everyone else. It is not their fault; don't treat them as if they are to blame. Other children may shun the child who has a behaviour difficulty, especially if part of the problem is hurting or shouting at others.

Set up situations where everyone can:

- celebrate small achievements

- discuss and understand how others feel

- have clear guidance on what is unacceptable and why.

All children need to know it is the behaviour that you dislike and not the child.

Ideas for managing behaviour in groups

- Try bringing children together who do not usually get on. There is often one child who is a target for another, and working together with them in pairs or small groups is better than always separating them. Help them learn to co-operate and get to know each other.

- Model how to play, talk, share. Some children don't know how to relate to others, or how to behave in an acceptable way. Throwing all the cups and saucers on the floor in the home corner, or worse, throwing them at someone else, may reveal a child who does not actually know how to go about this kind of play. He/she may just need to watch what the others are doing or copy you. Most children respond well to this sort of modelling, learning a new way to behave acceptably.

- Sometimes have a couple of smaller groups instead of one big one.

- Help the child to sit quietly and be occupied alongside just one other child.

- Give positive feedback for sitting still, listening and responding appropriately.

- Ask a colleague to observe the child's behaviour and yours.

- Talk to the child about what he/she likes and doesn't like about carpet time.

- Increase group numbers very slowly.

- Take care to give a positive message about small group work – it is not a punishment!

- Try to understand that unacceptable behaviour is often caused by inability to cope with the situation not by a desire to be difficult or irritate you!

- Try not to take the behaviour personally. Try to control your natural feelings of anger, frustration and disappointment.

- Bring the child to sit next to you and give them a job to do.

> Shouting, ridicule and rough handling by you are clear signals to children that this sort of behaviour is acceptable!

> Remember, if the group size exceeds 8, the fall-off in learning and attention for all children is substantial. Keep group sizes small when you can.

> Catch the children getting it right; praise the behaviour you want and try to ignore the behaviour you don't!

Of course, all children want to have their own way sometimes, but understanding, distraction or discussion, appropriate to the age and stage of development of the child, will always be more effective than punishment. A child who pokes and prods others will almost always respond to being given the responsibility of helping you. And it will have the added effect of occupying their hands!

In the Early Years Foundation Stage, working with children in groups of 2 or 3 benefits all the children in the group, as well as being an important strategy for children with attention and behavioural difficulties. Research tells us that group sizes of eight or less result in higher levels of learning.

Small group work done with everybody (not necessarily all at the same time) will ensure that children who need to do more of it do not feel they are being singled out. Make sure the small groups have mixed membership – it's not so profitable to have all the difficult behaviours in one group, and working with mixed groups helps all children to understand each other.

Structured play in pairs, such as rolling a car or a ball to each other, is a good place to start. This can be extended to threes, then fours, taking turns to roll and listening carefully for the adult to tell them who to roll to next. This will help with learning to wait, to pay attention to what is being said and to receive praise gracefully when they get it right!

On a day to day basis remember to:

- demonstrate the appropriate way to play with the toys and equipment

- try lots of simple games in pairs and small groups to help children get along with each other

- give instructions with visual prompts. Show them what you want rather than just saying it

- make routines and expectations very clear and consistent. You need to ensure that what you are asking is realistic and achievable for the child

- give instructions one at a time to begin with – complex strings of instructions will not work!

- instructions which you know are easy for the child to follow will give you more opportunities to offer praise and encouragement

- use pictures or objects to help a child to understand what is going to happen next.

> **Remember, young children aren't mind readers! Be clear about what you want them to do.**

A purposeful programme

If you are going to be successful in helping children with attention and behaviour difficulties, you will need to practise identifying and using targets. All difficulties, whether caused by a lack of maturity, a learning disability or a behavioural problem need to be broken down into a series of small steps, which can be made into targets, and achieved one at a time by the child. Achieving one target and being consistently praised for it will have a much more positive effect on a child than having a target which is too large, or too many targets at once.

For instance :

The problem: He/she gets very involved in activities and finds it difficult to stop when I ask them to do something else.

The target: He/she will stop and listen, and then do what I ask.

The strategy: I will give him/her an individual warning that it is almost time to stop, and s/he will hear the music for 'Clearing up time soon'.

The reward: I will praise him/her whenever they respond to the music.

The timescale: This may take several weeks, but by half term, I expect him/her to stop for the music on most occasions after a reminder.

Achieving targets and receiving praise will help to raise self esteem, and positive reinforcement works much better than negative comments. Don't be tempted to follow up your praise with a negative, such as 'You listened very well at story time, but you still wriggled during the singing.' Accept good behaviour and praise it for what it is, not for what you would like it to be.

> Concentrate on one behaviour at a time.

> Focus on the behaviour, not the child!
> Don't make it personal.

Higher self-esteem will help a child to relate to the other children in the group, make friends and succeed in the group. It is sometimes hard to praise one child when he does something which you expect to be the norm for everyone else. Remember you are not making comparisons, you are helping an individual to achieve a small step on the way to behaving like everyone else.

Other children may shun a child with a behaviour difficulty, especially if part of the problem is that he/she hurts others. Children need to understand that you will not tolerate unkindness or violence in or to any child, and you need to model appropriate recognition of small targets met, and small steps achieved. Sharing targets with the whole group sometimes helps children to understand and celebrate the achievements of others.

Remember, if your response to unacceptable behaviour is to shout, or punish the child with ridicule or rough handling, you are teaching the child that your behaviour is acceptable. Personal, Social and Emotional development will not improve if adults don't provide good models.

Singing their praises

Repeatedly using the same vocabulary for praise and correction will gradually lose impact, and very general praise or correction is also ineffective. Make sure your comments are clear and precise.

Simple, general praise sounds like this: 'Good boy/girl', 'Nice work', 'Well done.'

Precise, helpful praise sounds like this: 'Thank you for picking up the Lego bricks', 'I really like the way you have drawn that picture', 'That was a really kind thing to do, helping Naomi to put on her coat', 'You really listened well to the story.'

All children like to have attention, and if the only time they get it is when they have done something wrong then they will continue. If they get attention all the time for good things, there will be no need for them to try to gain it in less appropriate ways. There is no need for a great fuss. Just knowing that you are noticing good behaviour, describing what you like and praising it is enough.

'Well done for...'

'Great, I really liked...'

'You are really doing well with ...'

'What a good boy/girl for ...'

'Thank you so much for ...'

'You are such a good helper today, helping with ...'

'Great work! I really like the way you ...'

'I like it so much when you...'

'You are sitting so well! Look everyone at this good work/good sitting/ good playing!'

> **Be clear about what you like and don't like, using simple language, praise and modelling.**

)f mischief, or they have more energy than they can expend easily at
ery child is entitled to the odd misdemeanour, which can usually be
trouble. But children with real behaviour problems seldom have only
ir behaviour has probably been deteriorating over several years. They
rfect overnight, and there will probably be many behaviours you

Identifying the problem

ificult behaviours and decide where to start. Try asking yourself, and
with the child:

blem is the behaviour? Observe the child and see when, where and
haviour is happening. Sometimes observation will reveal patterns that
aging the behaviour.

oblem? – Is it the child, other children, adults?

o work together to deal with the behaviour consistently?

on one aspect of behaviour for one child impact on the rest of the
up or setting?

the behaviour to change? What do you hope to achieve?

ons of behaviour and change realistic?

> **Observe, observe, observe!**

roblem

y to answer these questions as a team:

- What is your shared description of 'unacceptable' behaviour? If you don't discuss this and agree on clear descriptions, your interventions will fail, and the child will be even more unsure of what is expected. It's worth spending plenty of time on this stage.

- What is the most difficult behaviour we have seen in this child? Does everyone agree on the most difficult behaviour?

- How many behaviours would you like to change? Which is the 'number one' priority?

- Is there any behaviour that you feel would be easier to change than others?

- Is there anything (organisation, time, reminders, clear choices etc.) that, if changed, might have a significant impact on the behaviours?

> **Catch the children getting it right; praise the behaviour you want and try to ignore the behaviour you don't!**

- Do we already praise everything we possibly can that this child does?

- What do we like about this child? What are his/her positive features, characteristics, interests which we could praise, use and build on?

What can we safely ignore?

Because you can't address all the behaviours at once, you have to decide the behaviour to target first, then agree how you are going to deal with the other behaviours.

The target behaviour

You have already looked carefully at the behaviours and talked about which ones you find the most difficult, disruptive or upsetting. Be strictly honest – you need to think carefully about your own attitudes, both individual and collective. You may need to compromise, but it is vital at this stage to agree the behaviours you are going to target.

It is also easy for the adults to get a real 'down' on a child, to scapegoat them and constantly feel that they are always naughty. Being singled out unfairly often exacerbates the poor behaviour. The spiral of deteriorating behaviour can also make you feel guilty or a failure in your job. Adults can end up feeling inadequate if they feel they are not managing a child or group of children well.

These questions might help you to decide where to start:

- Is the behaviour dangerous to the child or to others?

- If this behaviour happened in a different situation, would it still be unacceptable?

- Is it a general problem among the children in your setting, or does it only apply to a few, or even just one child?

- Is it disruptive to activities? Which activities?

- Do you feel annoyed, hurt, offended or frustrated when it happens?

- Might other children begin to copy and behave in the same way?

- Does it happen so frequently that you cannot cope with it any longer?

- What would happen if you did nothing?

- Do you usually ignore the same behaviour in other children? If so, why?

Now you have looked carefully at the behaviours you find unacceptable it should be easier to decide where to start. Are you going to go for the behaviour you find most difficult, or the one which you think will be easiest to change? Going for the obvious one may give you a quicker result, a better opportunity for giving praise, and an improvement in self esteem for the child. You will all then have the boost which success gives and will be spurred on to further efforts.

> **Start with one of the more obvious behaviours. Which is easiest to see and describe? Which one gives you all the most frequent problems?**

Xerox Global Print Driver PCL6

Driver Name:

An example of STEPS 1 and 2

Jimmy has never been expected to sit at a table for meals. He messes around with his food, eats little, and generally disrupts meal and snack times. He finds it really difficult to sit with the other children and causes problems for them at the table. How can we improve his mealtime behaviour?

1. Identify the behaviours:

This is not just one behaviour, but several, connected ones.

> **Plan one stage at a time.**

- he eats very little
- he won't sit with others at a table, keeps getting up
- he plays with the food and sometimes throws it
- he disturbs others and they follow his behaviour.

2. Look at each behaviour individually:

Not eating

- Does he behave in the same way at home? Talk with his parents, they may be having similar problems at home. If so, they may be glad of some help and be prepared to join in with your programme at home.

- Is he used to eating this sort of food? Children are seldom undernourished these days, and most children will eat when they are with a group. However, some children just 'graze', never eat a meal, always snack.

- Is he given other food when he refuses what is offered? Parents sometimes find mealtimes very hard to handle and give up trying! They find it difficult to insist on sitting at a table and eating what is on offer. And children are adept at getting what they want! They seem to know by instinct that their parents worry about them going to bed hungry, and that persistent refusal to eat will result in getting the food they want.

- Does he eat anything at all while he is in your setting? Look carefully at what and when he eats. Does he particularly dislike a few foods or does he just refuse most things? Does it matter that he does not eat much while he is with you, if he is eating at home?

Should you ignore the behaviour and let him do something else at mealtimes? This response won't help! He is using meal times as a challenge and you need to deal with the problem. Giving him something else to do avoids the main issue and rewards him for not doing what you expect of other children.

Not sitting at the table

- Refusing to sit at the table could be a symptom of many things. Watch carefully and note the exact behaviour. Try talking to him and asking why he doesn't want to come to meals. He might feel threatened at being expected to sit close to others. He may just not know what to do, how to use the cutlery, what the food is. He may be afraid that he will be forced to eat. He may not be used to sitting at the table at home; there may not even be space for one; or perhaps your situation is just too quiet!

Playing with food

- Playing with food is messy and upsetting, and inappropriate throwing of any sort has to be stopped immediately and firmly. All children need clear guidelines on behaviour at all times.

Disturbing others, who then copy him

- Disturbing other children erodes your whole community. It makes children feel insecure, and makes adults feel out if control! You can't be seen to accept it, and a structured approach will be appreciated by everyone.

So now you will be asking:

The answer is – you decide. Look at all the behaviours and decide where to start. You could start with the behaviour which is affecting the other children, or the one you as adults find most difficult, or the one that takes most time, or the one that makes most mess. You decide!

> **Tackle one thing at a time.**

For example, sitting down at the table could be the behaviour you choose to work on first. Trying to deal with playing with food, refusing to eat or disturbing others may not work if he can't sit on a chair! Dealing with one thing at a time is always easier, and your clear response will have an impact on the other behaviours.

Perhaps you have decided that you want him to just eat a little of something. It will need to be something he likes, so find out from his parents or carers what this could be. Get them to bring a very small packed lunch of something he likes (you may even have to start with crisps or biscuits). Once you have established the behaviour you want, your praise will usually stimulate an interest in extending his diet to more healthy items.

> The vital component of each of these strategies is to praise and reward the behaviour you want! We'll look at rewards later.

Slowly, slowly, step by step, with your support and praise from everyone, he will begin to enjoy getting attention for his behaviour.

> Give plenty of time for the behaviour to establish itself, and expect some regression to previous behaviours when he is tired, stressed or unwell. Don't be tempted to move to another behaviour too soon. Remember how long it has taken him to learn the unacceptable ones!

Whatever you choose to do, make sure that everybody, including the child, understands. Be clear that it is not a punishment for bad behaviour, but an opportunity to behave well.

STEP 3 – Clear expectations and small steps

When you have chosen your target behaviour, and made sure everyone knows what it is, you need to build up a programme in small steps to work on individually, making sure you observe carefully whether your ideas are working and how the child is responding. Remember, you will have setbacks. This does not mean the

whole thing is a failure, nor does it mean that it is not worth doing. It will probably mean that the child is testing you to make sure you really mean it, or that your steps or targets are too big and you have to think again.

What is 'unacceptable behaviour'?

Definitions of 'good' and 'bad' behaviour differ between individuals (adults and children). Children often respond quickly, on instinct and without considering the consequences. Younger

or less experienced children need to learn what is acceptable and what is not, and this needs practice, clear guidance, praise and good models.

Remember, children grow up in homes with widely varying expectations of behaviour. These are affected by culture, nationality, religion, gender and location. Different is not always worse! Behaviour that may be quite acceptable at home, may not be acceptable in a setting for large numbers of children. There are times when the safety or security of other children in the setting is at risk, damage might result, or children might be hurt. In these situations, we have to act clearly and consistently.

All the people who work in your setting must agree which behaviours are unacceptable, and how you are going to deal with them, and your response will differ according to the age, stage of development and situation of the children in your care.

Some behaviours generally accepted as undesirable are:

- hurting other children or adults
- doing something which may cause harm to the child him/herself
- destroying or damaging property or other children's work
- running, climbing or shouting in places where they might disturb or endanger others

- throwing things which are not meant to thrown, or in a place where it is not safe

- name calling or other verbal abuse aimed at children or adults

- swearing or using undesirable language to adults or children

- refusing a reasonable request from an adult

- tantrums, screaming or other uncontrolled outbursts.

> **Be clear about what is unacceptable. Describe it in simple words.**

You may have others!

How you deal with any of these behaviours will, of course, depend on:

- the age and developmental stage of the child involved and their level of understanding

- the length of time they have been with you and whether they have had time to learn the routine and what you expect

- the background of the child and whether appropriate behaviour has been learned at home

- whether this is a recurrence of a previous behaviour in the same child.

STEP 4 – Sanctions, punishments and telling off

In any setting, no matter how well regulated, there are times when children need to learn which behaviours are acceptable, and which need to be dealt with immediately. Strategies for improving self-esteem can only be effective if they are set in a framework of clear expectations, so your next step is to decide what the sanctions and rewards are to be. Having decided which behaviours you will not accept, you then have to decide between you how you are going to deal with them, and if the same sanctions are going to be used every time.

Will you:

- use a 'zero tolerance' policy for some behaviours?

- give warnings? If so, how many?

- increase the level or type of punishments for each further misdemeanour?

Some tips for success:

- Never shout at a child across the room unless there is real, imminent danger.

- Go to the child. Bend, kneel or sit down so their eyes are level with yours. Make sure they are looking at your face, and tell them calmly and clearly what they have just done.

- Tell them clearly that you don't want them to do it again.

- Use a firm voice, but not an intimidating one.

- Stay with the child and model or talk through the behaviour you want; how to play with another child or to use the toy etc.

- When you leave them, watch from a distance, where they can see you.

- Let the child know from your expression that you are pleased with the improvement.

What if they do it again?

- Return and repeat the procedure as before. This time add that if the behaviour continues, they will have Time Out (a period in a quiet place with nothing to do). Be clear about what Time Out means, indicate the place (the particular chair, cushion, mat where they must sit).

- As before, stay with them for a while before withdrawing to a distance.

And again?

- Now you must follow through. You absolutely must do what you have said.

- Explain clearly what you are doing and why. 'You have done (X) again, and now you must go and sit on the chair until I say you can come back to play.'

What is Time Out and how does it work?

The Time Out procedure is used after the child has had two or three warnings about a behaviour that you have all agreed is unacceptable and is the focus for your plan.

- the child is taken to a previously identified chair/mat/cushion/step

- they must sit there quietly for a previously agreed number of minutes (usually only one or two minutes) with a sand timer if you have one

- they must be quiet and sit still

- if they get up they are returned to the Time Out place

- if they shout or scream, they are ignored

- at the end of the time they must return to the activity and demonstrate that they can play appropriately

- they should also apologise to anyone they have disturbed or upset and restore order if they have thrown or tipped up equipment.

Time Out helps a child to realise that you are unhappy with what they have done; that they are responsible for their own actions and behaviour, and that they should not do it again.

'Why is Time Out better than simply removing the child from the situation or activity?'

Removing a child from the situation and still allowing them to go and play with something else, or go to a different area will not give an opportunity to reflect while they can still see others playing without them.

Tips for Time Out

The rules for 'Time Out' must be observed every time if it is to be effective:

- Your Time Out chair, or area should be clearly identified. Always use the same piece of furniture, in the same place.

- The Time Out place should not be outside the room, just away from the rest of the activities.

- Make sure you can see the child, and they can see you.

- Give the child no attention at all while there, not even eye contact.

- Make sure everyone knows that Time Out is not meant to be a punishment, it is time to calm down and reflect.

- Don't leave them there for too long. As a general rule, use a maximum of one minute of Time Out for every year of the child's age.

- When the time is over, invite them back into the group, saying that you are pleased to have them back and how still and quiet they have been while they were thinking.

- Don't keep going on about it, he knows why he has been there.

- If appropriate, ask them to apologise to any child who has been hurt, but then forget it.

- If the Time Out decision triggers a tantrum, throwing or other physical disruption to the room, leave the mess until the end of the Time Out, then ask the child to help you clear it up. There is nothing more frustrating for a child than having to watch a well behaved and well intentioned classmate putting things right, leaving them with no chance to make amends.

- Make sure everyone follows the same process. Particularly when Time Out is supervised by more than one adult, make sure you all agree on chances, isolation times and reintegration procedures.

What if the child goes from one thing to another, continually misbehaves, or repeats the target behaviour endlessly?

When you start to intervene in difficult behaviour, it often gets worse before it gets better! A child with a behaviour problem has been developing it for some time, maybe for years. The behaviour may have become second nature to the child and their family. The child may also be testing whether you will keep to the agreement on punishment or Time Out. They may have had plenty of experience of threats and promises which have never been kept. You need to be determined. Stick to the plan and give it time. If a child continually misuses a particular activity, even between sessions of Time Out, then you could deprive him of it for the rest of the day, but make sure all staff in the room know about it and why. Don't make a big fuss, just remove the child to something else and calmly tell them why.

> Stick to the agreed plan! Remember, it will take time and they will test you!

Focus on observation

Before you can decide whether to be concerned about a child's behaviour, you must be sure that he or she really has a problem. Sometimes it is only too easy to think a child has real difficulties, when he/she is just having a bad day, or even when we are having a bad day!

How do we go about finding out the difference?

The key to sound judgement about difficulties and to overcoming them is observation.

> Observation is the key to understanding.

What is observation?

Practitioners are observing children all the time:

- to see how they are developing

- to check their emotional and social responses – who is upset, who is unwell, who needs help, who needs to be challenged a little more

- to see how children are behaving, and if any of them need extra attention, support or guidance in their behaviour or in socialisation.

When it becomes clear that a child is having difficulties or causing disruption, it can be very useful to do a structured observation to find out what is really happening. In a busy setting it is possible to get a partial or skewed impression of what is going on, and this can lead us to think that the behaviour is happening more often that it really is, or that a particular child is always responsible for the disruption, noise or mess.

How do we do this sort of observation?

You are trying to find out how often the child's behaviour causes concern. Be careful here; it is very easy for every member of staff to be watching an individual child like a hawk and marking down every move they make. This can alter the child's behaviour and produce a false picture of the problem. You are also trying to find out how much of the day is spent in the unacceptable behaviour. Adults sometimes have a feeling that the behaviour is happening all day every day. However, when careful observation is carried out, it is frequently found, that out of a five-hour day, only 10 minutes is actually spent in the unacceptable behaviour, and looked at in perspective, you will certainly feel better about altering 10 minutes of difficulties than five hours of them!

> **Get a clear and accurate picture, check it with everyone.**

Now decide who is going to do the observation.

Do you want to use a key person, or would it be more objective to use someone who does not know the child well, and therefore doesn't have pre-conceived ideas?

When should you do it and how long should the observation last?

Detailed, structured observation is time consuming and tiring. It takes high levels of concentration and self discipline. Short periods of observation (15 minutes at a time) over several days will be more productive and manageable.

What time of day would be most appropriate?

Plan your observation periods to cover all sorts of times of day and all sorts of activities. It's important to observe the child at times when they are not having problems as well as times when they are. Outdoors, indoors, quiet times, free play, group times, snack, story and discussion times can all be included, and remember to include different days of the week.

> **Record what you see, not what you think you see, or what you think should be done.**

What should you be looking at and looking for?

Record as much as you can of what you see and hear. Remember to include the well behaved, kind, thoughtful, obedient behaviours and actions as well as the problems. Of course you will record any times when the worrying behaviours occur, but remember to 'catch them getting it right'! When the worrying behaviour occurs, try to remember and record what triggered it, what the child did and what happened next.

> **ABC**
> **Antecedent**
> **Behaviour**
> **Consequence**

This is called the **ABC** of behaviour management.

A – the antecedent (what happened just before)
B – the behaviour (how the child behaved, what they did)
C – the consequences (what was done to deal with the behaviour)

Recording the times when the child behaves acceptably is very important. You will need to know these, partly to get a realistic picture of the problem, partly to find ways to praise and reward the child, and situations which may help you to understand what is happening.

How should you record the observation?

A notebook, with a new page for each period of observation, and a new line for each new incident of recorded behaviour is a useful system. Record the time of day, the activity and the children present as you begin each period of observation. You may find it helpful to record in five minute blocks, so you can locate the time when any particular behaviour happens. See the example overleaf.

General guidance on structured observation:

- The observer should not be doing anything else – you may need to engage extra adults to cover their work.

- The observer should not openly follow the child around. Obviously she/he will need to be able to see them clearly, but not be so close that behaviour is affected.

- The child should not be aware that s/he is being watched. Knowing that s/he is being watched is sure to make a child 'play to the audience'.

- The observer is not there to deal with the behaviour when it happens. If necessary, they should ask another member of staff to intervene.

- Never set up a volatile or 'risky' situation purposely to see what will happen, and then use it as evidence against a child.

- The observer should record exactly what they see – like a camera, not an interpreter.

What should we do with the knowledge we have gained?

These observations will become the basis for your more detailed plans, which you will use to help the child to modify their behaviour and change their reactions.

The ABC of behaviour management

When we talk about managing behaviour, we really mean that we want to reduce the behaviour which we dislike, and help children to behave in the way we want – a way which will give them more chance to learn and make good relationships with others.

We have already talked about the kinds of behaviour which prevent children learning, and about observing a child to discover whether you really have a problem, and if so, what it is. We have not yet addressed the reasons behind the behaviour and what causes it.

You now need to look at your observations, and if necessary observe the target behaviour in more detail, so you can discuss the immediate cause. You need to find out why the behaviour happened at that time, what actually happened and what happened afterwards.

Time spent discussing these aspects is never wasted. You will have a better understanding of the child and the behaviour, and have some chance of reducing it.

1. Take your structured observations and identify the key problem behaviours.

2. Now draw up a schedule for recording the behaviours. This schedule will have days, dates, times, and spaces to record the A, B and C of the key behaviour(s).

3. Now begin to log each time a target behaviour happens. Initial and date the observations, especially if there are lots of staff.

Only write what you see yourself, not what other people have told you, or what you think of what happens. Concentrate on the target behaviour and write as much as you can of what happens as you see it. Don't rely on your memory!

Here is an example.

Name: Jake		Problem behaviours:	1. Grabs toys, will not take turns. 2. Refuses to obey instructions from adults. 3. Runs away when reprimanded.		
Day	Date	Time	What happened before (**Antecendent**)	The **Behaviour**	What happened next (**Consequence**)
Monday	11th Jan	10am	Jake was sitting on the floor playing with the train set. Deepak approached and put his hand on the engine.	Jake pushed Deepak over and stamped on his hand. Jake grabbed the engine and said 'Mine'.	Deepak screamed and ran to an adult. Jake ran from the area, looking upset and still clutching the engine.
Monday	11th Jan	1.30pm	Jake outside, wanted red bike which Jenny was riding, told by Marcie (teacher) that he must wait for his turn.	Pushed Jenny off bike, got on and rode away.	Marcie fetched him and asked him to apologise. Jake refused, ran away and climbed to the top of the climbing frame.

Of course your detailed record will have many more incidents in it. You will need to spend a week or two on your observations, even if the behaviour is happening very frequently. In this way you can establish the pattern of behaviour properly and really understand what is happening, but even from these two incidents some things are becoming clear:

- Jake has not learned how to share, wants his own way and is prepared to hurt another child in order to get it. However, he does seem to know this is not the approved way to do it!

- He has learned that this behaviour usually works. The other child lets go and cries. Jake does seem to have learned that he might be in trouble for what he has done, hence the defiant looks, and running away.

- What should you do? Jake knows something about his behaviour. At present it is working, so he still continues with it.

- There are four things he needs:

   1. Help to understand clearly that he is not allowed to hurt others. The methods on pages 39–41 (warnings followed by Time Out) would help here.

   2. Help to understand that hurting others will not get him what he wants – he will not be allowed to keep the toy.

   3. Models of positive play with other children, how to share things, people and experiences.

   4. Plenty of practice, and praise for getting it right!

Remember to consider both the age and developmental stage of the child. Make sure your sanctions and expectations are realistic. Take everything you know about the child into account when deciding on your strategies, the number of warnings, length of Time Out, number of targets etc.

Strategies for specific behaviours

Take one step at a time

When you feel you have managed to reduce or modify a particular behaviour sufficiently and think it is time to start trying to work on something else, you need to begin the observation cycle again. Start with new charts and new observations to identify the next behaviour to target.

> One step at a time.

As things start to improve, return to your ABC!

It is possible to have some overlap by starting the second lot of observations while implementing the programme for the previous behaviour, but don't try to do too much at once.

> **Don't try to do too much at once, don't move on too quickly.**

Tried and Tested tips

- You know all the children in your group, so if you anticipate a problem, take steps to stop an incident happening. If you know that something always upsets a particular child, and sets off difficult behaviour, do your best to either remove him/her from the situation before it happens, or warn them in advance and support them through it.

- Small steps, and plenty of time, will help a child to learn what to expect and how to cope. Don't worry too much about academic achievement while you are working on behaviour. Concentration, attention to what is going on and helping a child to manage their own behaviour must come first. This underpins successful learning.

- Involve the child in your discussions. They need to feel they are part of the process and that they have a share in the success.

Some suggestions to help you on your way to success

For a child who finds it difficult to complete a task:

- Ensure that you know what he/she can already do before you try to move on to the next step. There is no point in trying to write your name if you can't hold a pencil!

- Make adult directed tasks short, so the child does not feel too pressured, and so they are almost guaranteed to complete it.

- Break it down into small steps that they can do one at a time.

- Sit opposite the child, with your head at their level, and make good eye contact, especially when you are introducing something new.

- Make absolutely sure the child understands the task and knows what is expected by:
  - demonstrating or modelling – doing the first part of the task yourself
  - watching and helping the first few times
  - being available to help when they need it
  - staying close by, perhaps working alongside with another child, so you can reassure and encourage.

- Offer small rewards such as a change of activity between steps so they don't feel that you are just adding extra things on. A task can feel never ending to some children and a quick break makes all the difference. Extend each step little by little until the whole task can be completed.

- Do some of the task yourself, perhaps by putting in alternate pieces of a puzzle, making sure the child puts in the last one so that you can legitimately give praise for finishing the task. As time goes on, you will do less and they will do more so eventually they do the whole task.

For a child who finds it difficult to follow routines:

- Give a warning to the child a few minutes before you tell the other children what is going to happen. 'We are going to go to the hall in a minute, so start to put your game away.'

- Give an opportunity to finish what they are doing, by telling them when something new is about to happen. 'We are going to music in five minutes, you've just got time to finish that brilliant painting.'

- Make a pictorial timetable of what is going to happen throughout the day, so that all the children know what to expect. You could use individual cards for each activity, so that they can be fixed in place with Velcro each morning in the order of the day.

- Have copies of these pictures for those children who need it, so that they can be given a clue card before the general warning. They will then know what to expect and will not be so surprised by changes.

- Make sure there is adult help at each change of activity to offer explanation and support.

For a child who finds it difficult to sit in a group:

- Make sure that the activity of the group is not too difficult, or beyond their understanding.

- Allow the child to sit to one side to help them feel less confined. If all the other children are sitting close together on a carpet, give them a small square of carpet to sit on, not too close to the others. If they are all on chairs at a table, sit between him/her and other children to help them feel secure.

- Work in a much smaller group, perhaps only two children to begin with, making it larger by one or two children over a period of time, until it becomes easier. Use plenty of praise.

- Offer the child a small soft toy or puppet to hold, as long as they don't use it to disturb other children (or themselves).

For a child who finds it difficult to stay still for any length of time:

- Try not to remove a child from a group because he/she is misbehaving. This may be just what they want, so you are giving a reward for doing something you do not want to happen.

- Use a timer, or perhaps have a selection of egg timers which take increasing lengths of time to run through. You can then say, 'Try to sit still until the sand has run through, or the timer goes off, and then you can...'
Start with a shorter time than you know they can sit, and increase the time very slowly, until eventually they can sit as long as the others. This has the double effect of increasing concentration, and rewarding it without the need for disruption to the rest of the group.

- Let the child start by joining the group for the last few minutes, perhaps just for the last song, so they can leave at the same time as everyone else. Then you can give praise for sitting still until the end of the session. Again the time is lengthened bit by bit, but working backwards!

> **Children learn through imitation, example and expectation. Role models are very important!**

- Obviously, you can choose whichever strategy is most appropriate for the child, or use a combination of them to suit your circumstances.

For a child who often hurts other children:

- Try the ideas in 'Observation' and 'The ABC of behaviour management'.

- If he/she often picks on the same child, try to put them together in a twosome with an adult to work on an activity. This may help them get to know each other, and to get along together better.

- Tell them clearly every time how much it hurts to be hit/bitten/pinched.

- Give plenty of praise every time you see them playing well alongside others without causing any problems.

> **Always be seen to be fair. Listen before you judge!**

- If they lash out without thinking when someone takes something from them or tries to join their play:

  - Work with him/her to play alongside other children, on their activity. Move on from this to playing with one or two others, on a co-operative activity, not with their own favourite things. Help with sharing by giving them and another child similar things, and encouraging them to swap from time to time. At an appropriate stage, start to divide things between the two children so they can practise being fair.

  - Always listen to their side of the story, and try to be fair.

For a child who has tantrums which seem to be beyond his/her control:

- Try to identify what the triggers are for this kind of behaviour, and if at all possible, avoid them!

- Do not try to force the child into doing something which is obviously distressing for them.

- Don't give in for a quiet life! Be consistent, fair and firmly quiet.

- Wherever possible ignore a child who is having a tantrum, put him/her in a safe place and act as though they are not there!

Case Studies

The case studies on the following pages are illustrations of situations from a range of settings. They have been included as examples, for practitioners to discuss and think about. You could use them in the following ways:

- to just read and consider
- as discussion material for staff meetings or other training
- for ideas and strategies to help you manage children in your setting
- as 'cautionary tales' to save time and energy by learning from the work (and even the mistakes) of others!

> Remember, it's not their fault! Most children want to behave well.

N.B. all names in the case studies have been changed.

Case Study 1

The problem

A day nursery asked for help from a SEN adviser in making an application for funding for extra support for a 4-year-old child with, in their words, 'severe behaviour problems.' The manager said that they were considering excluding him, but did not want to upset his mother because she too had many problems, and William had been in their nursery since he was six months old.

> Be sure of your evidence, be specific.
>
> Try to use clear descriptions, not 'fuzzy' generalisations,
>
> such as 'always', 'all the time'.

The adults felt they had tried everything, and were getting nowhere. They described William as 'naughty', never sitting still for group or circle times, hurting other children and behaving inappropriately with toys and equipment, throwing and breaking things on a regular basis. Staff also listed a bad-temper, tantrums, screaming and shouting 'all the time'. They were convinced he had ADHD and they felt he needed an extra Nursery Officer to accompany him all the time so he could be kept safely away from the other children to avoid disruption.

The assessment

The adviser visited the setting for a morning to observe William and see what was going on. When she arrived he was sitting on a chair by himself, crying. He had grabbed someone's leg when he should be sitting quietly and had been removed from the group.

> Is it 'wrong', 'naughty', or just a behaviour learned in a different situation?

Later William sat at a table and drew 2 pictures with felt pens. He moved away and completed a 12 piece jigsaw puzzle unaided. He went to the construction area and had started to build a crane, when another child sat beside him and tried to take it from him. William hit the child and snatched his model back.

The problem

Two members of staff came running, one took William and moved him away, one took the other child and cuddled him. Later when many of the children were playing boisterously under the large desk in the room, William joined in. Immediately he was shouted at across the room and warned that he would have to have 'time out'.

The morning continued in this way, no one took any notice of any of the children when they were occupying themselves well or sitting still, but as soon as William (particularly William) put a foot wrong he was reprimanded by all the staff.

The Plan

The adviser and the manager met to discuss the problem, and the adviser suggested that the thing the nursery should consider first was not an extra member of staff, but a course for the staff in positive behaviour management and a change of policy for handling the behaviour of all children in the setting.

The manager agreed to fund the training. Everyone on the staff attended a 2 hour session, with plenty of practical ideas, and a subsequent discussion of their roles and responsibilities. Three weeks later the adviser returned to see how the ideas had been implemented. The manager was very enthusiastic about developments. William, she said, was a different child, and would be moving into his primary school the following term without any of the difficult behaviour reports he would have had before. The staff were all delighted in their own success, and all the children (including William) were getting plenty of praise when they got things right and appropriate handling for any difficulties.

The Future

William may have temporary set backs in the future, but discovering that praise and reinforcement work much better than punishment will help the nursery staff to feel much more in control.

Case Study 2

The problem

Nicholas, who was subsequently diagnosed as having ADHD, was attending his local infant school. He had been in their Foundation unit since he was three, and was known to have difficult behaviour. Staff had used all the usual sanctions, but Nicky continued to have really severe temper tantrums and to kick out and scream at other children when something upset him.

New situations or people sometimes trigger extreme responses.

The history

The staff in the Foundation Stage had already worked to help Nicholas avoid the triggers that usually set him off. They understood that he found it difficult to sit too closely to the other children in a group and arranged for him to have a separate small mat instead of having to sit on the carpet. They tried to ensure that he could go to a quiet area by himself if he was getting upset. In this way they managed to reduce his outbursts to a minimum, while giving him the opportunity to calm down when things were tough for him. He was no angel, but they managed him well.

However, as transfer to Year 1 approached, they felt he was not yet ready to sit for any length of time, or to see an activity through to the end, and were giving him help to improve on this.

New challenges

On transfer to Year 1, Nicholas' behaviour became more difficult. He had found the change hard to handle. His tantrums became more frequent and certainly a great deal more spectacular.

New challenges

The school decided to operate a zero tolerance policy and every slight misdemeanour was punished. His teacher insisted that he must sit with the other children on the carpet, as she thought that he should learn to conform. Nicholas was not able to cope with new expectations in a new place. His behaviour deteriorated and he spent a great deal of time in the Head's office where he was berated and expected to complete his work. Time Out was usually for a good half hour, and was often followed by a lecture on proper behaviour. Nicholas began to dread going to school and started refusing to go. The worst of his behaviour was transferred to home, his parents found it really difficult to cope with him and really needed him to be at school. The staff were finding it increasingly difficult to manage and often sent for his mum to take him home.

> **Be patient, things sometimes get worse before they get better. Don't change your strategy because it doesn't work instantly.**

The LEA Behaviour Support service and Educational Psychologist were involved and a programme was agreed. However, the zero tolerance policy was continued. Eventually there came a day when Nicholas was brought to school in the car and refused to get out. His mum, having decided she was having no more nonsense, took him from the car and carried him towards the classroom kicking and screaming. On the way (and by accident) a staff member was kicked very hard, sustaining some bruising. Nicholas had injured a member of staff! An emergency meeting was called and Nicholas was excluded. His mother was distraught; the school felt that despite all their hard work they could no longer accommodate his needs. Nicholas was placed in another school where he joined a Nurture Group, with staff who use positive behaviour strategies, work hard on raising his self-esteem, and are helping him to learn to express his anger and frustration in more acceptable ways.

A reflection

What went wrong here? Was this a child who was beyond help and totally out of control, or could a different response have helped him to control his own behaviour without so much confrontation? Certainly his degree of difficulty was extreme. The school had a good reputation for its behaviour policy and management. Everyone felt they had failed. What could they have done differently?

Case Study 3

The history

Four year old Ryan had a very difficult early life and was now in Local Authority care with his three brothers. They have an excellent, caring home in a foster family. Ryan has uncontrollable bursts of violent behaviour at home, but apart from being disruptive in group times at pre-school, he has not shown any violent episodes.

New challenges

Ryan has recently moved into the Reception class of his local primary school, and is finding it very hard to settle into the new routine. He has extra help, in the form of a special needs teaching assistant, who is helping him on a one-to-one basis for part of the day. He has a very short attention span, finds sitting with the other children very difficult and needs a great deal of support to complete an activity. Although Ryan is a little behind his peers in some aspects of learning, he has good spoken language, and is able to learn new concepts as long as he is sure of what is expected of him, and is clearly shown what to do.

The assessment

On the day he was observed, Ryan was working with his support worker at a table with no other children present. He had been shown how to copy a two-colour pattern on a pegboard. The pattern was one red peg, followed by two blue pegs. Ryan was helped to do the first two rows and then asked to complete the board. Unfortunately, it was a board with 100 holes and there was a large tin of pegs of six different colours. This activity was Ryan's work for the second half of the morning, before lunch. He was finding the job tedious, to say the least, and having been given help for the first 2 rows, was left to his own devices. He was however being watched, and continually being told to hurry up or get on with it.

Ryan looked around the room, and was obviously attracted by some of the other activities going on. Many of the other children, having finished their mornings work, were working independently with self chosen activities, and what they were doing looked much more interesting.

Ryan frequently asked if he could go and build blocks, play in the house, do a painting, and several times got up from the table. He was told every time, 'No, you have to finish this and then you will be able to play.'

> Make tasks manageable.

and the response...

Eventually, the observer intervened. She asked the teaching assistant if she could try to help Ryan to finish the activity. Obviously it was important for the observer to act sensitively. She must not say that Ryan can leave the task, that would undermine what he had already been told.

The observer asked Ryan if she could do a row of the pattern. This he willingly agreed to. Then she asked him if he would help her to sort out the colours they needed to finish the board. Together, they made a pile of red and a pile of blue pegs. Next they took turns to put the pegs in, first Ryan did the red and the observer did the blue, then they swapped. Soon they were halfway down the board and not long after they were on the last row, which Ryan completed on his own. This all took 15 minutes. Triumphant, Ryan showed his board to everybody who would look. He went to get his special sticker, to put on his chart of 'My finished work' and at last Ryan could play.

Just as he walked towards the blocks, the teacher said 'Time to put everything away and get ready for lunch!' How he finished the session without a major tantrum, we will never know, but credit to Ryan, he didn't explode with frustration!

> Make sure they are successful.

A reflection on what happened and why it went wrong

The activity was too big and complex. Although well within his capabilities, there was too much of it. Perhaps a board with 25 pegs would have been more appropriate. When Ryan showed a lack of interest, he needed encouragement and assistance. There were no opportunities given for him to be praised, and he needs this all the time.

He could also have done far more useful things in the hour or more he had spent on the pegboard task. He could have gone to play with the big blocks, and built them into patterns, he could have made patterns in the paint. He could then have completed lots of things, been praised for completing them and enjoyed himself into the bargain. Instead, he was fed up; frustrated and above all deprived of the one thing he was working towards, and had been promised – time to play.

It is vital to think in advance of what you want to achieve with a child. If you want to teach them to do something specific and you know that their attention span is short, plan several different short activities which will reinforce the same intention, and don't forget to build in some fun too!

> Build in regular breaks, especially for boys.

Boys in particular need regular breaks from concentrated activities. Children can generally be expected to concentrate on one directed activity for about the number of minutes of their age in years before they need a short break (a chat, a physical movement, a relaxation of muscles etc). And many children will achieve more if they work on several different directed activities in an hour, not just one.

The history

Isabel's behaviour was causing some concern. She lives on an isolated farm, with no near neighbours and no siblings. Three mornings a week, she attends a playgroup which serves several rural villages and the outlying farms.

The problem

Isabel is a robust little girl, very physical and muscular. She is also very determined to get what she wants. She has had no competition for toys or attention during the first three years of her life and her current way of behaving is to run across the room, trampling over everyone in her way to get to what she wants, without seeming to even notice the damage in her wake! She sometimes hurts other children and does not seem to realise that their crying has anything to do with her. Some speech and language delay means that Isabel often refuses to sit with others in group situations, preferring to go off into the home corner to play by herself.

> **Find out all you can about a child's background.**
> **Listen to parents and make expectations realistic.**

However, Isabel does love snack time! In response to an adult calling 'Snack time,' the children come and sit down, each on an individual carpet square. The adult takes the register, invites children to tell the group what they have been doing, and they sing a song or two before the milk is given out. When each child has finished their drink they can take a biscuit or piece of fruit from the plate. Isabel hates sitting in groups, but she loves snack! She is also very observant. She knows the snack will not appear immediately! She waits until the discussion and singing are over and the drinks and food come. Then she appears and tries to help herself to a snack. The practitioners feel that if they allow Isabel to do this, the other children will copy her behaviour. So they say she can't have a snack because she didn't come and sit down with the others. This always results in a tantrum.

The assessment and some suggestions

An LEA adviser observed Isabel for a morning and suggested a slight change to the routine. When the children were called for snack this should be given straight away to everyone, before the discussion and singing. Isabel should be encouraged to sit at the edge of the group and should also be given her snack as soon as she arrived.

> **Sometimes you have to do something special to help an individual. The other children are usually very understanding!**

The staff were very doubtful about this, because the routine was working for everyone else, and they felt that Isabel should be doing what everyone else did.

Another suggestion from the adviser was that Isabel should be ignored when everyone else was sitting down, or perhaps given some one-to-one teaching for her speech and language problems. She should be called for snack when they were put out and given it when she sat down.

The outcome

Three weeks later, the adviser returned. Isabel was standing in the middle of the room in a full blown tantrum. All the other children were eating their snack. The staff had decided that only total obedience would be accepted. The suggestions for action had been rejected, and Isabel, although she had come to sit down at the point when the snack was being given out, had been told that she could not have it unless she came to sit down when all the others did, sometimes as much as 20 minutes before the snack came out.

Some thoughts

- Children who have behaviour difficulties (and many others who don't!) need immediate rewards.

- Sometimes we may decide to change a routine for the whole group to make things easier for one child. We may decide that the payoff is worth the change.

- Sometimes we need to make different arrangements for different children. These may need explaining to the rest of the group, and will need to be agreed among the adults.

> How many other children are just as frustrated by the wait, but are less prepared to show it? How could you find out?

- We need to remember that sometimes we can be so keen to be consistent and so insistent on order and rules, that a child's individual needs may be forgotten! It takes real professionalism to decide when to bend or break our own rules.

- We must also ensure that we meet children's needs in all areas. This setting may be in danger of meeting Isabel's language needs while neglecting her behavioural needs.

and some questions

- What would you do and say if you were the adviser on your second visit?

- How do you think Isabel will cope with school? What will the Reception teacher need to do?

- What would you advise the playgroup staff to say to Isabel's parents about her problems?

- How could you persuade a reluctant colleague that a previously agreed routine should change to accommodate the needs of an individual child?

Partnership with parents

As an Early Years practitioner you are already an expert in working with parents. But you may find that including a child whose behaviour and attention span differs from your usual expectations can be quite a challenge.

Parents who are worried about their child's behaviour are very often afraid you will not want the child in your setting. Establishing a good relationship of trust and understanding is vital. Children will pick up very quickly on any hint of tension between you and their parents.

Remember that parents may feel fearful and even tearful as they hand over their child, possibly for the first time, to someone they don't know very well. Their worry and concern may appear aggressive or defensive. Try to be understanding and find a way of helping them to trust and have confidence in you. Remember, their own experiences of school may not have been happy ones, and all parents want the very best for their children, even though they may not be able to express this.

Never forget that parents are a vital source of information and experience of their child. Listen to them, ask for information and work to gain their trust and confidence. Sometimes you may have to tease out information, waiting for the right moment, collecting information over time, and understanding that parents may be protecting themselves and their child. They may be wary of your questions, or on the defensive.

You could re-read pages 9-13 to remind you of how to make a good start.

When working with parents, remember to:

- work slowly, clearly and sensitively with their child to help build a relationship with their family

- try not to be critical or judgmental

- keep parents informed at all times; involve them in the programmes and targets, ask their advice, collect information about how things are going at home

How would you feel if this was your child? What would you feel like doing and saying? How would you want to be treated?

- highlight the child's strengths as well as any difficulties, report on these regularly to parents

- try to greet the parents every day with a report of successes, however small; concentrate on positives wherever possible; keep a home/setting diary where both sides note progress and significant events

- listen to what they have to say – let them go first! The information parents give is vital and may be the key to successful intervention in your setting

- draw up a good, consistent, readable behaviour policy, show it to all parents and be seen to use it! Show your intention to be fair, just and consistent.

Hopefully you will have met the parents of all your children before they come to you, either in your setting or on a home visit. You will naturally have asked parents whether they have any worries about their child's ability to settle in, to make friends, to co-operate with adults and other children.

If a difficulty in behaviour has been very severe, and parents have asked for advice beforehand, perhaps from their health visitor, try to find out what advice has been given, what strategies the parents have used, and how successful these have been. Always take account of which strategies have worked for them as this will provide a useful starting point for you.

Working as a member of a team

Including a child who has behaviour difficulties can involve working with a range of outside agencies to help you deal with difficulties and help the child as much as possible.

Get to know who these agencies are, make a note of contacts and phone numbers, and establish what kind of help they can provide for you, the child and his family.

Work hard to make a success of working co-operatively with other staff, and accept and appreciate that people have different skills, experiences and attitudes, as well as the different roles and responsibilities they have in your setting.

> Building a multi-disciplinary team of support for the child and their family will be vital in their attempts to come to terms with behaviour management.

- Understand and respect the roles and responsibilities of each member of staff
- Share your commitment to a common goal
- Communicate effectively with each other
- Make the most of the skills and experiences of everyone involved.

The ways in which you work together every day in your setting are the same ones you will use to ensure that you are an integral part of a multi-agency team, offering coordinated support to the child and their family.

There will be targets and strategies to work on together, and it is crucial that the targets complement each other, are consistent and are fully understood and agreed on by everyone who is working to make sure that the child gets the very best help available.

> Emphasise co-operation, not competition between agencies!

Effective multi-agency working will ensure that:

- the child and family get consistent messages

- approaches blend well together and help the child towards agreed and planned common goals

- professionals and practitioners make the most of a wide range of training, skills and experiences of people from different sectors

- everyone is aware of the effects of the child's difficulties in different areas of his/her life and the implications for learning

- the most effective support is available.

Multi-agency working involves time, effort and commitment. Plan to share information efficiently and set aside time to prepare for and attend multi-agency meetings. It will be worth the time and effort and is an essential part of good practice.

Remember, you and the parents are the ones who will need to put all the ideas into practice and to make them work for the child. Your observations and experience are essential to the picture of the child; what you have to say is very important and helps the other members of the team to see how their strategies are working and how the child is being helped to access learning and develop the skills they need.

For more information on working together, visit **www.earlysupport.org.uk**

Who's who in multi-agency working?

- First and most important – the parents

- Your Headteacher, or Nursery Manager. They will be able to listen to you, and support you when the going is tough.

- The Special Needs Co-ordinator for your setting.

- The Educational Psychologist.

- Members of the Local Education Authority Special Needs team or Behaviour Support Team who have been allocated to work with your setting, or the individual child and their family.

- Social Services may have some involvement especially if the child's behaviour is so difficult at home that respite care is being considered.

- The Paediatrician from the local Child Development Team.

- Any therapists who may be involved.

And what might you need to do?

- Attend meetings called by various agencies for advice and information.

- Attend meetings in your setting to make sure that all the things you are trying to do are working.

- Negotiate and agree targets and prepare plans to help the child to meet them.

You will need to keep observations of the child, records of what you are doing, how well it is going and how the child is benefiting from the intervention of the agencies involved. Record keeping arrangements must be in place in your setting for any child with additional or specific needs. It is crucial that you keep these records well and that you write down relevant information as soon as possible, so when you are asked to provide a report for any of these meetings, you will have all the necessary information to hand to make your report relevant and up-to-date.

> **Try to see meetings as a valuable source of support and information, not as a waste of time! Make sure you are well prepared.**

Paediatrician
A hospital or community-based children's doctor, often specialising in children with special needs.

Educational psychologist
Responsible for offering advice and support to schools and for assessing the learning needs of children.

Speech and language therapist
Working often from a community health centre, specialist centre or from a child development centre at a hospital, speech and language therapists offer advice and therapy to build communication skills. Therapy may be direct one-to-one, or small group work, or maybe in the form of advice and support to parents, either individually or at a group.

Specialist pre-school teaching support or Portage worker
Specialist early years practitioners providing structured learning for babies and young children, often one-to-one in the child's home, and providing advice and support to parents.

Child development assessment centre staff
Either community or hospital-based service providing specialist assessment, diagnosis and ongoing support for babies and young children with special needs and their families.

In addition there will be:
Social Services professionals
HomeStart volunteers
Occupational Therapists.

The team may also include parent partnership workers providing independent parental support. In addition, parents may receive advice and support from local or national voluntary organisations, such as local branches of the National Autistic Society.

Early years practitioners include:
Setting Managers
Key Workers
Special Needs Co-ordinator (SENCO)
who ensures the child has the best possible support from the team and an Individual Education or Learning Plan (IEP).

Further help and key contacts

You are the person who is working with the child every day, and you are in an extremely good position to give information to the other agencies. Do not be daunted because you are being asked by specialists to provide them with information. They need you and your knowledge of the child to help inform their own reports and discussions. Without you, they would not know half as much, so be confident and trust your professional judgement. You are a very important person in the child's life, you really can make a difference, and everyone involved will appreciate you for it!

Where to go for further help

First of all ask advice from your Local Education Authority. You are entitled to contact them if you are a parent, school or a Private, Independent, or Voluntary provider of Foundation Stage Education.

They should be able to put you in touch with their:

Special Educational Needs Service

The Educational Psychology Service

Behaviour Support Service.

Look for Local ADD/ADHD Support Groups, who can provide information and give you details of meetings etc. Their work is usually aimed at parents, but they may also welcome interested professionals. They can usually be accessed through the local Volunteer Bureau, or Citizen's Advice Bureau who will have the addresses and phone numbers. They will help even if you do not have a diagnosis.

ADDISS

The National Attention Deficit
Disorder Information and Support Service
PO Box 340
Edgeware, Middlesex
HA8 9HL
www.addiss.co.uk

The Challenging Behaviour Foundation

The Old Courthouse
New Road Avenue
Chatham
Kent
ME4 6BE
www.challengingbehaviour.org.uk

Resources and websites

For your bookshelf

SEN Code of Practice on the Identification and Assessment of Pupils with Special Educational Needs (DfES)

ADD/ADHD Behaviour Change Resource Kit;
by Grad L Flick Ph.D

ADHD the Facts;
by Mark Selikowitz

Step by Step Help for Children with ADHD;
by Cathy Laver-Bradbury

Managing Difficult Behaviour in the Classroom – A Pocket Guide for Teachers;
by Grad L Flick Ph.D

ADHD in the Young Child: Driven to Redirection;
by Cathy Reimers, Ph.D, and Bruce A. Brunger

Shelley, The Hyperactive Turtle;
by Deborah M. Moss and Carol Schwartz
The story of a bright young turtle who's not like other turtles. Shelley moves like a rocket and is unable to sit still for even the shortest of periods. Because he and the other turtles are unable to understand why he is so wriggly and squirmy, Shelley begins
to feel naughty and out of place. After a visit to the doctor,
Shelley learns what 'hyperactive' means and that he needs
to take special medicine to control the wriggly feeling.
With the love, support and understanding of
family and friends, Shelley fits right in.
For ages 3–7.

On the Web

On the internet there are countless websites at your disposal through any search engine. Here are a few central contacts to get you going:

Mencap: The voice of learning disability **www.mencap.org.uk**

The National Association for Special Educational Needs **www.nasen.org.uk**

The National Autistic Society **www.autism.org.uk**